JULIA WARNER

BEGINNER'S GUIDE TO MYSTICAL SPELLS AND RITUALS

A Step-by-Step Journey into Mystical Spells and Ritual (2024)

Contents

Beginner's Guide to Mystical Spells and Rituals

"Easy and effective Rootwork, Conjuring, and Protection Spells for Healing and Prosperity."

Introduction

During times of immense hardship, I stumbled upon Hoodoo and recognized the profound potential embedded within this mystical practice. Throughout my life, I have delved into various spiritual traditions, yet none have resonated with me quite like Hoodoo. Originating from African-American communities, primarily in the southern regions of the United States, Hoodoo magic may be a relatively recent form of sorcery in the grand scope of history, but its enduring impact has forever shaped the destinies of countless individuals worldwide.

While it may not currently enjoy the same level of popularity as it once did, Hoodoo magic continues to hold a significant role in the lives of its practitioners, often referred to as rootworkers or root doctors. However, it is crucial not to be misled by these titles. Hoodoo transcends the mere manipulation of roots, herbs, and spices; as you will soon discover within the pages of this book, it encompasses a far broader and more profound realm of knowledge and power.

My Personal Experience Awakened

I've had a personal connection with Hoodoo since my early years. While my parents adhered to Jehovah's Witnesses, Hoodoo magic always held a special place in my heart. It fascinated me in a way that was hard to put into words.

My grandmother was a staunch believer in Hoodoo. I can vividly recall sitting and observing her concocting potions in her home, diligently gathering ingredients from wherever she could find them, and playing with intricately designed bottles and vials she had collected over the years.

However, I struggled to fully comprehend Hoodoo myself. Despite my introduction to it many years ago, I hadn't yet embraced the practice and opened myself up to it. Looking back, I now realize that the timing simply wasn't right. In fact, that moment didn't arrive until about a decade ago when I found myself in my apartment during some of my darkest days. My emotions churned within me despite all the tears I had shed.

I was trapped in a toxic and explosively violent relationship. In retrospect, I see that my ex-partner and I were both battling our inner demons, and while we may have loved each other in our own way, we were not meant to be together. It was during one particularly intense fight that I began to grasp this truth for the first time. He left our apartment to stay with a friend, leaving me alone in my dimly lit space, slumped over the kitchen table, with the only illumination coming from a streetlight across the road.

I was lost, confused, and uncertain about what the future held for me. It was in this very moment, with my head in my hands, that the allure of Hoodoo gently beckoned to me. Initially, I was taken aback, but that surprise soon gave way to curiosity and fascination. All the fragments of knowledge I had gathered over the years slowly started to connect in my mind in a way they never had before. Curiosity began to consume me.

I retrieved a book that my grandmother had passed down to me many years earlier from the bookshelf and spent an hour or so flipping through its pages, not quite sure what I was searching for. Eventually, midway through the book, I stumbled upon a recipe for a happiness potion. I chuckled to myself. Could it really be that straightforward?

I reminisced about my grandmother all those years ago. I held deep love and respect for that woman in my life, so I thought, if she believed it worked, then maybe I should too. It took some time and a peculiar nighttime walk to Bronx Park, but I managed to gather all the necessary ingredients. I scoured the apartment for odds and ends I could utilize. The book was old, with a torn spine and missing pages, but most of it remained. It was a book of protective spells that described roots, herbs, spices, and more.

Just under an hour later, the potion was prepared, and I recited the spell inscribed within the book's pages. I also took a few moments to write down my intentions on small pieces of paper, folded them up, and attached them to the potion vial. I then sat with this arrangement for about half an hour, meditating on my intentions.

Initially, I wished for an escape from my suffering, and that was undoubtedly true. My sadness felt overwhelming, and I simply wanted it to end. This was my primary intention, but it gradually receded into the background, making way for something deeper.

I felt a sense of peace and calm, but I also felt resolute. There was a lasting moment of stillness that seemed to stretch on and on, during which I felt determined. Motivated. Driven. I knew I was stuck in a rut, but I sensed a burning determination within me that believed I could move forward if I put my mind to it.

At the time, I thought it was merely a moment of realization, an epiphany of sorts, and to some extent, it was. However, I now understand, in light of my subsequent experiences over the years, that it was a form of magic. Since then, time and time again, I've been able to tap into this wellspring of power, a magic that resides not only within me but within all of us.

What is Hoodoo Magic?

At its essence, according to the dictionary's definition, Hoodoo represents an art form employed to invoke, materialize, and trade both physical and spiritual energies. It serves as a form of sorcery used to generate and attract prosperity, well-being, increased fortunes, and better relationships. Additionally, it acts as a conduit for shaping your intentions and providing a sense of purpose that empowers you to conquer any challenges or obstacles encountered in life.

Hoodoo comprises a collection of spiritual customs, traditions, and beliefs rooted in the Black African communities wrongfully enslaved by North Americans and Europeans over the past three centuries. It serves as a means for individuals to welcome supernatural forces into their lives with the aim of enhancing them.

The term 'Hoodoo' first appeared in written records around 1870, although its true origins remain uncertain. As the spelling suggests, it is believed to have derived from 'Voodoo,' although these two practices differ significantly, as we will elucidate later in this chapter.

Regrettably, over 12 million people were subjected to slavery and transported from Africa to North America (now the United States) between the 16th and 19th centuries—an exceedingly traumatic experience whose repercussions still reverberate worldwide through people like us today.

It was within these enslaved African communities, which evolved into African-American communities, that Hoodoo took root, ingraining itself in the culture and eventually evolving into its present form. Nevertheless, a form of Hoodoo was previously practiced in Africa, initially regarded as a religion but later transforming into a form of magic. Let me provide some perspective on this matter.

In the 18th century, Black slaves in America did not have access to the same medical care as those in European-American communities. Consequently, Black communities had to establish their own support and healthcare systems, devising ways to care for themselves—both the enslaved and the free—covering psychological, emotional, and spiritual needs.

With no alternatives, they depended on the knowledge and spirit of those around them who were experiencing similar hardships. They found solace, support, and knowledge within this practice of care, communication, and unity, which enabled them to process their trauma and seek healing amid their dire circumstances.

Since enslaved individuals hailed from diverse African cultures, societies, and ethnic backgrounds, Hoodoo emerged as a unifying force, blending magic, love, respect, and community from various sources that might otherwise never have converged. In a beautiful way, this amalgamation can be seen as a form of magic in itself.

Consequently, modern Hoodoo represents a fusion of religious and magical practices that coalesced under extremely trying conditions, rendering it one of the most potent forces known.

Central African regions exerted significant influence on Hoodoo, with evidence suggesting that about 40% of all enslaved Africans came from these central areas, particularly the Bantu-Kongo regions. This influence is evident in Hoodoo practices, which exhibit clear connections to the Kongo cosmogram and Kongolese beliefs and rituals.

Another substantial influence derives from the Western African region, introducing elements such as the magical mojo bag. Given that many ships involved in the slave trade traveled to and from North America via the West African coast, which served as the hub for the trade's management and organization, it's unsurprising that a substantial number of individuals from this region fell victim to slavery. There are also discernible traces of magical influence from West African Muslim communities that resided in these areas during the era of the slave trade.

Today, Hoodoo is practiced within the more subtle aspects of society. Practitioners are often referred to as 'root workers' or 'root doctors' because of their emphasis on working with herbs, roots, and plants. Although it is commonly called 'root working,' it's crucial to remember that this represents just one facet of Hoodoo practice.

What sets Hoodoo apart from other Western or European magical traditions, and what makes it appealing to many, is its lack of necessity for summoning or establishing relationships with other spirits or entities. While the 19th century introduced a considerable Christian influence, Hoodoo practitioners do acknowledge the existence of a deity of sorts, yet there is not a pronounced emphasis on this deity.

The Hoodoo God is a gender-neutral entity, neither inherently good nor evil, despite Hoodoo's distinct notions of good and evil. This God serves as the supreme creator of the world but remains unconcerned with human affairs. Lesser entities and spirits are responsible for intervening in these matters, one of which is the Boo Hag. The Boo Hag, as a collective term, denotes spirits that exist to haunt and terrify the living. They possess magical and spiritual powers capable of causing or curing diseases, predicting the future, or aiding in finding lost items.

Considering Hoodoo's origins, such beliefs make sense. For example, African-American populations in Indiana refused to enter a specific location, believing it to be haunted by the spirits of Black individuals who had suffered violent deaths. This is attributed to the work of the Boo Hag.

However, not all spirits are malevolent or rooted in pain, misfortune, and terror. Some spirits provide protection from suffering, promote peace and tranquility in tumultuous situations, or reside within the elements, like the MIA, the West African water spirit.

Nevertheless, despite the potential for a comprehensive exploration of Hoodoo's history and its spiritual realm, the paramount aspect to remember is that it originated from suffering and remains deeply embedded in the hearts and lives of our ancestors. This is where its true power emanates.

The Links Between Voodoo and Hoodoo

Hoodoo magic and Voodoo magic, despite sharing some core similarities, are distinct practices with their own unique characteristics. It's essential to clarify this primary distinction in your understanding. While they have certain commonalities, they are not synonymous, although they are undoubtedly interconnected. In popular culture, Hoodoo is often used to encompass various forms of Native American or African cultural magic, while Voodoo is recognized as a religion and a magical tradition. Both have been influenced by African and European elements.

However, there is a significant difference in their associations with Christianity. Hoodoo has loose ties with Catholic Christianity, whereas Voodoo has connections with Protestant Christianity. It's crucial to note that practitioners of either practice are not required to be devout Christians.

Voodoo magic is primarily a religious practice originating from countries like Haiti, with links to West African populations. Within Voodoo, one must follow a path that leads to ordination in the religion, with leaders overseeing the magic rituals. A multitude of deities, gods, entities, and spirits must be revered and honored for the practice to be conducted correctly.

In contrast, Hoodoo imposes no such requirements. Practitioners are not obligated to believe in or follow any specific gods; they are free to worship any deities they respect or believe in. There is no hierarchical structure with overseers, priests, or other ordained individuals who hold authority over practitioners.

Hoodoo lacks the rigid structure often found in other religions. It is a practice that individuals discover and connect with within themselves for personal benefit, without the aim of serving a greater purpose or worshiping an entity. Therefore, Hoodoo can best be described as a form of personal magic.

In contemporary society, the terms Hoodoo and Voodoo are frequently used interchangeably, albeit incorrectly. This misunderstanding persists among those who are not well-informed about these practices. In reality, modern

Hoodoo, especially the "non-African" variant, draws on some elements of Voodoo magic but is perceived by its practitioners as a more Christianized version of the predominantly practiced Voodoo in places like Haiti.

It is essential to dispel the misconception that Voodoo is exclusively used for malevolent purposes. Hoodoo often falls into the same category for many due to similar misunderstandings, but both Voodoo and Hoodoo can be harnessed for benevolent purposes such as healing and prosperity. However, like any practice, they can also be misused for malicious intentions.

In brief, it's important to clarify that Hoodoo and Voodoo are distinct practices, despite some shared elements. Both encompass diverse variations, but in this book, our primary focus will be on Black Hoodoo, originating from African-American communities. Interestingly, Black Hoodoo has roots in African Voodoo but has been influenced by European culture due to its emergence during the era of African enslavement in America, resulting in a fusion of the two cultures, including Christian influences.

As you'll discover later in this text, many Hoodoo spells incorporate recitations from the Psalms and Bible passages, reflecting strong ties to Christian teachings. Another branch of Hoodoo is referred to as 'White Hoodoo,' which denotes practitioners without African ancestry. While they may not have African origins, these individuals are still non-white and did not experience enslavement by other Africans or descend from African heritage.

Due to Hoodoo's historical context, it remains a magical practice primarily associated with Black individuals.

Chapter One: Hoodoo in the Modern World

In the realm of hoodooism, it's crucial to grasp that every action you take is intricately intertwined with the divine plan of God. Whether your deeds are virtuous or flawed, they are bound to God in some way, and the consequences thereof are inevitable. You will inevitably receive what is due to you.

In our contemporary world, we all encounter challenges and tribulations at various points in our lives. These issues encompass a wide spectrum, including financial struggles, relationship complexities, dealings with landlords, career hurdles, health concerns, and every other facet that impacts us, regardless of its magnitude.

Life, without a doubt, has an uncanny way of throwing unexpected obstacles and trials our way. The key lies in discovering how to navigate these situations for the sake of our own physical and mental well-being, as well as inner tranquility.

Hoodoo stands as a methodology, a process, and an art form that can offer solutions to the questions that plague you. It serves as a spiritual practice that facilitates reconnection not only with your core self but also with your history, ancestry, and past experiences.

In times of darkness, hoodoo acts as a guiding light, warding off lurking shadows on the horizon, just beyond our vision.

My personal journey with Hoodoo has been marked by progression and redemption, which has inspired me to document it, in the hope that it might encourage you to open your heart and mind to the marvels of Hoodoo.

This undertaking is by no means simple. The history of Hoodoo is extensive and originates from a place of hardship and suffering. However, one thing in life remains constant: the presence of discomfort. Rather than resisting it, it is time to make amends with this discomfort by embracing and transcending it. It may sound daunting, but this book is here to guide you towards achieving this.

You have already come a long way, and holding this book in your hands at this moment is a clear indication that you are prepared to take the next stride. I firmly believe, at the core of my being, that you seek the same enlightenment

I once did, and you are now on the verge of a remarkable discovery.

You're on a quest for answers, searching for a clear path to follow. Your determination is unwavering as you yearn to rediscover a connection with your inner self, instincts, and spiritual essence. It's time to cultivate trust in your inner wisdom, unlocking your full potential in any circumstance. It's the moment to bring your desires and aspirations to life and start living the life you've always envisioned.

While to some, this may appear as an insurmountable idea, it is not. There has never been a time when an intentional practice like Hoodoo has been more significant or potentially transformative in the lives of countless individuals. Acquiring knowledge about this practice can open numerous doors in your life and assist you in overcoming any potential barriers holding you back.

In the upcoming chapters, we will delve into the intricacies of Hoodoo concepts, sharing the wisdom passed down through generations. We will delve into the history and origins of Hoodoo, unveiling its roots and stories. We'll also explore the principles and guidelines, offering guidance on how to become proficient in this practice and integrate it into your daily life.

Consider this book as a beginner's handbook—a stepping stone in the right direction, providing enough information to set you on a solid path toward self-discovery. This isn't about fantastical magic or miraculous effects seen in movies; it's about intentionality. It's about aligning your mind, spirit, and soul, facilitating healing, processing past traumas, and safeguarding yourself from future challenges. It's about finding serenity during the toughest times so that your inner light can shine brightly once more.

If you've been grappling with darkness and adversity for the past few years, or even longer, flipping through these pages offers you the chance to kindle a guiding light. With this act, you ignite the spark that kick-starts this journey in the most auspicious way possible. The candle has been lit.

How to Use Hoodoo in the Modern World

Hoodoo emerged from a necessity born out of the anguish and suffering endured by Black individuals. Consequently, it is a form of sorcery exclusively wielded by Black practitioners. In the past, it found application in a variety of contexts, which included:

- Fostering joy within families and communities.
- Enhancing one's fortunes and improving the likelihood of favorable circumstances.
- Alleviating sensations of agony and distress.
- Mending the wounds of trauma, both physical and emotional.
- Providing a shield against forthcoming perils.
- Administering retribution upon those responsible for causing pain.

These circumstances continue to afflict many of us today, and you may have encountered them personally. In an era marked by turbulence, it appears that Hoodoo will remain pertinent.

Should you aspire to practice Hoodoo and wish to integrate its enchantment into your life, you must establish a profound connection with its history and origins. This involves empathizing with the agony, suffering, and sense of unity inherent in its roots. It may be an uncomfortable journey, fraught with pain and traumatic recollections from your own past that you'd rather avoid, but you must be receptive to the ancestral summons, channeling their energy.

We will guide you through this process step by step, and it's essential to reassure yourself that there is no need for fear or trepidation. Many before you have trodden this path, and many will follow in your footsteps. Open your spirit, and together, let's embark on this journey.

With this in mind, you should now be prepared to take your initial strides into the realm of Hoodoo. It's time to rekindle your connection with this mystical tradition and witness its advantages firsthand. As you reconnect with this historical power, take a deep breath, turn the page to this new chapter, and let us commence.

Chapter Two: Getting Started with Rootwork/Hoodoo

The psychic witch lives in a constant state of enchantment, perceiving everything as mystical and comprehending that the universe is comprised of boundless opportunities and potential. While others perceive a wall, the psychic witch perceives a door." — Mat Auryn

When I initially embarked on my journey to connect with my inner magic, I experienced a blend of emotions. I felt excitement and curiosity about the unfolding journey, but it would be disingenuous to deny a hint of fear. After all, what awaited me on this path? What if I unintentionally tapped into some profound, dark energy or encountered spirits burdened by trauma and suffering, from which I couldn't escape?

These concerns did cross my mind, but deep within my heart, my intentions remained clear and pure. I sought inner peace and a guiding light to navigate my personal darkness. My quest began during some of my life's darkest moments, and I was determined to push through my insecurities and explore further.

However, it's vital to remember that you need not tread this path alone.

There are others on a similar journey, some just starting out and others who will begin soon. I, too, once stood where you are now. Additionally, your ancestors stand behind you, those from whom you descended, many of whom were practitioners of Hoodoo and may have even witnessed its origins.

When embarking on Hoodoo practices, the first step is to acknowledge this reality. You must open your mind, soul, and heart to the magical guidance before you. If you wish to ascend through magic, you must invite it in. While this may sound simple, it's a nuanced process that won't happen overnight.

Regrettably, the act of opening your mind cannot be strictly taught; it is a journey of overcoming obstacles as you encounter them. Opportunities will present themselves, such as during particularly stressful periods. It's when you become mindful that these stressful or painful moments can be opportunities to connect with Hoodoo magic that you'll begin to understand its potential. It all begins with mindfulness.

For instance, if you find your relationship is in turmoil and you're facing difficulties, it's easy to fall into patterns of arguing or attempting to score points. Perhaps you're the type of person who conceals negative emotions, suppressing them until you're on the verge of exploding.

It's during challenging times like these that you must remind yourself of the power of Hoodoo magic and what it can offer. It all begins with intention. Regardless of your actions, the aspect of your life you're working on, or the spells you're casting, their effectiveness hinges on your intentions. For now, concentrate on how Hoodoo magic can assist you.

There must be a reason you picked up this book and a reason you wished to explore Hoodoo magic. Let this guide you in opening yourself to the possibilities.

When you embark on your Hoodoo journey, this openness should be your primary focus. In the following pages of this book, starting from the next chapter onward, we will delve into various conjuring, protection, and healing spells, as well as explore the substances and natural products with Hoodoo properties.

Preparing for Your Journey

We've explored the mindset aspects required to prepare yourself for your Hoodoo journey, but now let's delve into the practical side of things. While Hoodoo primarily involves connecting with the supernatural, there are tangible actions you must undertake, such as gathering and utilizing various objects and materials.

Most of these items are simple and natural, akin to what African-Americans had access to during the 16th Century. They include plants, candles, leaves, pieces of metal, and other mystical artifacts like divination cards or totems. Personal concerns also hold significance in spells, particularly when the spells or potions are intended for specific individuals. These concerns encompass items such as hair locks, nail clippings, blood, bone fragments, or other bodily fluids. It's worth noting that acquiring an actual piece of bone from someone is not the expectation. Such spells were historically used to aid those who suffered in transitioning peacefully from the physical realm to the spiritual one.

Nonetheless, your focus should shift towards building a collection of natural products and personal concerns from individuals you wish to cast spells upon, as well as suitable containers. Some common items to gather include:

- Glass vials and bottles for potion storage
- Purses and fabric pouches for powders and ground materials
- Candles of varying colors and designs
- Matches or a lighter for lighting candles or burning spell components
- A pen and paper (or a dedicated Hoodoo notebook) for recording spells and intentions
- A variety of plant roots and natural herbs
- Stones, minerals, and crystals
- Divination tools like incense, pendulums, or tarot cards
- Oils, wax, amulets, charms, clothing, incense, and pendants
- Hair, bodily fluids, or personal concerns from either yourself or another person

In this context, I highly recommend acquiring a special notebook for documenting your Hoodoo practices. This notebook serves as a repository not only for spells and intentions but also for your personal reflections and experiences. You can jot down your emotions, the effectiveness of spells, or considerations for future endeavors. This written record is invaluable, as it contributes to your growth as a practitioner, enhancing your skills, conjuring abilities, and casting proficiency, thereby enriching your Hoodoo experiences manifold.

As you advance in your spellcasting journey and develop preferences for specific types of spells and potions, you will naturally become more familiar with the ingredients you require. Nevertheless, it's prudent to remain open to discovering potential materials that may augment your practice.

With your materials in readiness, you are poised to commence your Hoodoo journey.

Chapter Three: Introducing the Art of Conjuring

"If individuals do not confront the imminent danger, malevolence will be the one to reach them first. I conducted extensive experiments for more than a year, exploring various spells and methods within Hoodoo magic, attempting to discern what was effective for me and what was not. Regardless of my attempts, I consistently returned to the same place, using similar types of spells. These were essentially conjuration spells, also known as manifestation spells.

Different beliefs exist regarding the capabilities and limitations of these types of spells, but fundamentally, the power and intent behind them remain constant, allowing for diverse applications. To conjure or manifest means to materialize something that does not presently exist in your physical reality through intentions, thoughts, willingness, and belief.

Nonetheless, this does not imply that you can simply close your eyes and conjure a million dollars to materialize in front of you, neatly packaged in a shiny briefcase. The physical world has constraints preventing such occurrences. However, you can manifest a million dollars in your life in alternative ways, like manifesting financial security and comfort.

To conjure something in your life means to cultivate a mindset that can bring it to fruition. You actively engage in the process of conjuring your desires and inviting them into your life. Throughout your life journey, you might contemplate conjuring:

- The desired relationships
- Your dream career
- Financial stability
- Your dream home or car
- A sought-after promotion
- The realization of long-held aspirations, such as writing a book or completing a marathon

The possibilities are limitless, bounded only by your imagination. In my own life, I harnessed the power of Hoodoo to manifest the focus and creativity necessary to write this book. I protected and facilitated my healing from past relationship trauma. I invoked good fortune during job interviews when approaching new clients, and while meeting new individuals. In moments of stress, anxiety, or overwhelm, I employed Hoodoo to restore my mental equilibrium, discovering innovative solutions to surmount challenges and difficult situations. All of this was achieved through the efficacy of Hoodoo conjuration spells.

Conjuration, in essence, entails casting a magical spell or incantation. In Hoodoo, it involves establishing a connection with the spiritual realm, enabling supernatural forces to enter your life and exert a positive influence. This could encompass manifesting good luck, safeguarding yourself from harm, and more.

The specific desire you seek to fulfill is inconsequential. Hoodoo serves as a pathway to transform your intentions into reality, with the assistance of supernatural forces, spirits, and entities. Casting a spell entails establishing contact with these entities, communicating with them, and conjuring their presence into your life, depending on your objectives.

So, how does this process work, and how can you cast conjuration spells? Let's delve into a detailed example of the Hoodoo conjuration process and explore various ways to integrate these spells into your own life.

Imagine waking up one day, filled with boundless enthusiasm. You are well-rested and brimming with energy, eagerly anticipating a fantastic day ahead. In this exuberant state, you contemplate your goals for the day. To ensure you achieve these objectives, you take a moment to cast a spell for good fortune, enhancing your luck in all situations you encounter.

By casting the spell, you send a message to the universe's supernatural forces, summoning their assistance in your endeavors. As the day unfolds, you find yourself in increasingly favorable circumstances.

Perhaps you receive an awaited email, have a long-awaited meeting with your boss regarding a promotion, or a client responds positively to your proposal. These are the supernatural forces subtly orchestrating events behind the scenes, aligning everything as needed, often in ways too intricate for us to fully grasp.

Throughout the day, your thoughts remain focused on your goals, your mind determined to bring them to fruition. Any encounters, objects, or experiences that aid your progress toward these goals are met with gratitude and compassion. This guidance from supernatural forces ensures you are consistently in the right place at the right time, extending their influence beyond your immediate reality.

Conjuration magic need not be confined to subtle, positive purposes. If, for example, you are in a friendship that has been marred by hurtful actions, such as infidelity, spreading rumors, or tarnishing your reputation, you can invoke supernatural forces to address the issue.

Magic can be used to conjure a protective shield, heal emotional or physical wounds inflicted by the situation, or even redirect negative energy back toward the source, offering a taste of the consequences of their actions in the hope of imparting a valuable lesson.

Conjuration, at its core, involves summoning spirits to aid you in your life's journey. The manner in which you summon these spirits determines their purpose and how they will assist you. As later chapters will elucidate, this typically entails rituals, magical practices, and the utilization of ingredients and spell components.

From influencing individuals to fall in love with you, unlocking new opportunities, ensuring protection, fostering creativity, or alleviating pain, Hoodoo magic presents an array of solutions. With this understanding, you are equipped to embark on your journey into the world of Hoodoo and rootwork."

Chapter Four: Rootwork Spells for Conjuring and Manifestation

One thing you will quickly discover is that although the preparations for a spell may seem intricate, the actual execution of the spells themselves will prove to be quite straightforward.

But for now, let's put aside the theorizing and delve into the practical aspects of this book. With an open mind and a sincere desire to acquire these techniques and conjure Hoodoo energy fresh in your thoughts, it's time to establish a connection with this power and integrate it into your everyday life.

Keep in mind that certain spells and their required components might appear a bit intricate, and the process of amassing these items may take some time. Nevertheless, it's worth noting that many of these components can be used interchangeably across different spells. Once you have access to a specific component, chances are you'll be utilizing it for many years to come.

Now, allow me to guide you.

Incense: The Most Common Method of Conjuring

Assembling spells can sometimes be a challenging endeavor, particularly when you need to gather all the necessary ingredients. However, there's a simple way to cast a small conjuring spell at any moment, and that's by burning incense.

The market offers an abundance of incense varieties, and you can almost treat the spell as a form of meditation. All you require is an incense holder, preferably with an ash catcher, and your choice of incense.

Place the incense in the holder, light it, and sit with it for a few minutes. The longer you sit and essentially meditate with the smoldering incense, the more potent the spell and your intention will become. Simply sit, inhale the fragrances, and consciously attempt to connect with the Hoodoo power that resides within you and the universe.

While you sit and take deep breaths, remain as present as possible and gently steer your thoughts toward your intentions. Reflect on what you desire and consider various approaches to achieving it. Don't force rigid reasoning; instead, let your instincts flow and observe what comes to mind. Be as adaptable as water. Allow your thoughts to surface and let go of conditioned thinking patterns.

For instance, you might initially contemplate ways to increase your happiness and motivation at work, but as you delve deeper, you might realize that you're actually in a job you don't truly want, and your real aspiration is to pursue a more fulfilling career. Embrace such realizations as manifestations of Hoodoo magic rather than dismissing them as wishful thinking.

Now, let's explore some types of incense that can aid in conjuring and enhancing your focus and intention:

- Palo Santo is an excellent choice if you seek healing in your life. It is believed to elevate your energy vibrations and soothe your body.
- Frankincense is ideal for reducing stress and gaining greater clarity. If you're feeling lost, this incense can provide the clarity you need.
- If you aspire to achieve success and prosperity, consider burning Star Anise or Cinnamon incense to align your mind with making optimal decisions in this realm.
- Lavender serves as the incense of balance. When seeking calm, clarity, and inner peace for setting and discovering intentions or reconnecting with yourself or the Hoodoo source, this incense proves invaluable in clearing the mind and remaining grounded during turbulent times.
- For a deeper connection to yourself, the Hoodoo source, or the universe, Copal incense is the choice. It facilitates transcending or deepening your existing spiritual connections.
- If you desire a versatile incense that attracts a wide range of energies, Cinquefoil is an excellent option. While not overpowering, it serves as an uplifting incense, perfect for maintaining motivation if you're already in a positive state.

The strength and impact of incense spells can vary significantly. Sometimes, the effects may appear subtle, while other times, they can be life-changing.

Much depends on the individual experience, the specific incense chosen, and your current state of mind.

However, if you're in search of something more potent, consistent, and dedicated, you'll want to explore the spells outlined below, which are relatively beginner-friendly.

The Luck Draw Mojo

The Luck Draw Mojo ritual is employed to draw wealth into your life, whether it's by increasing your good luck or attracting favorable circumstances. For instance, when you're bidding for a project with a new client and you want to set your sights high, or when you're seeking a salary increase from your employer, this spell can assist you in effectively securing the financial outcomes you desire.

Ingredients:

- A red flannel pouch
- Magnetic sand
- A clove of garlic
- A lodestone
- Some sugar
- Some whiskey

To perform this ritual, place both the lodestone and the garlic inside the red flannel pouch, and pour a shot of whiskey into it. Seal the pouch and sprinkle magnetic sand and sugar on its surface. Finally, sew the pouch closed. Throughout this process, make sure to vocalize your intentions clearly.

The Serenity Spell

Life can often seem tumultuous, even during the most favorable periods. This is why many of us find it essential to allocate some time to discover our inner tranquility, to reconnect with a centered state of mind, and to generally prioritize our health and overall well-being. A perfect way to achieve this is by dedicating some time to conduct a serenity ritual, and it's surprisingly straightforward.

Ingredients:

- 12 white candles

Wait for a night when the full moon graces the sky and then proceed to illuminate all 12 candles, forming a circle around yourself. Sit in a comfortable position for as long as you desire. While seated, concentrate on your breath and immerse yourself in the present moment, grounding yourself. Allow the stress, worries, and anxieties to dissolve into nothingness as the moonlight and the encompassing universal energy purify you and your essence.

A Spell for Protection

Every comprehensive Hoodoo magic manual should include a safeguard incantation, as it stands among the most potent and universally applicable spells. Whether you're bracing yourself for a challenging conversation, navigating emotionally taxing circumstances, enduring difficult times, or simply seeking to safeguard your well-being and mental space, a protective spell can wield remarkable influence.

The good news is, this spell is remarkably uncomplicated to enact. You won't require any special ingredients or components; just yourself and the right words. Simply recite the following incantation silently within your mind or aloud whenever the need arises:

"Pater noster dei sanctorum. Maria Bella Angelo rum. Beautiful Mary slumbering. In a dream, the infant Jesus came to her. My dear, I dreamt of your arrival at the trial. Adorned with golden crowns, you were lifted high, while thorns took root beneath you. Your words ring true," answered Christ to your mother. Anyone who chants this thrice in an open field shall harbor no fear. Water, Thunder, and Lightning.

Feel free to repeat this spell whenever you require the shield it provides. As discernible from the cursive nature of the incantation, it exists to instill courage within you, irrespective of the challenges you confront, reassuring you that you're under the protection of entities and spirits greater than yourself.

A Spell for Passion

Do not mistake this for a love enchantment. A passion incantation serves as a means to enhance the bond and ardor within an already-established relationship, preferably between you and your romantic partner.

Ingredients:

- 3 drops of Lavender Oil
- 3 drops of Hot Sauce
- Pieces of Orris root
- Whole peppercorns
- Three cups of rainwater

Executing this spell is straightforward. Furthermore, you can adjust the scale of it to your preference. You can create as much or as little as you wish, provided you adhere to the ingredient ratios mentioned.

Combine all the ingredients in a bowl and stir. While stirring, direct your focus towards the heat of the hot sauce (the spicier the sauce, the more potent the spell), and concentrate on the sensations of temperature and texture. If there are any scents, they should be your focal point.

Once everything has been thoroughly mixed, take a portion of the mixture and sprinkle it at the front entrance of your house or at the entryway to a room or apartment. Ensure good coverage, and don't forget to apply some on the pathway. This will compel lovers passing through this entrance to be influenced by the heightened passion evoked by the supernatural forces you've invited to collaborate with you.

With that, we conclude this chapter. At this juncture, you've initiated a lovely collection of spells that you can tap into whenever you need to connect with the Hoodoo source. These spells should help you gain clarity in connecting with your intentions and defining them, assisting you in any situation or circumstance you may find yourself in.

Now, let's proceed to something even more potent.

Chapter Five: Rootwork Potions

"Everyone agrees that the Bible is the most powerful spell book in the world."

As you continue your journey into Hoodoo magic, the final stage remains firmly entrenched within the mystical realm of the craft. However, this time, the focus shifts towards the influence of elixirs and other enchantments. These mystical practices delve deeper into the world of rootwork and offer insights into what one can anticipate from such an undertaking. Feel free to select those that resonate with you as a starting point, yet don't hesitate to explore uncharted territories and expand your horizons.

These potions and rootwork formulas have been handed down since the inception of Hoodoo, serving as a gateway into this mystical realm. However, it's important to note that simpler and more intricate recipes exist, so embrace this wisdom and plunge into the depths of knowledge.

A Potion for Happiness

If you're seeking a method to elevate your spirits, foster a more positive mindset, and channel your focus toward achieving more productive outcomes, this elixir holds the potential to be of significant benefit.

Required Ingredients:

- A small container, preferably one with a cap or lid.
- Dried and crushed dandelion.

- One tablespoon of powdered oregano.
- One tablespoon of powdered cinnamon.
- One tablespoon of powdered thyme.
- Seven pine needles.

Combine all the specified ingredients within the chosen container, sealing it securely. Next, position yourself facing the East, holding the container in your hands as you proceed to enact the spell. Recite Psalm number 7 a total of seven times, which goes as follows:

"O LORD my God, I seek refuge in you; save me and deliver me from all those who pursue me,

lest like a lion they tear my soul apart, rending it in pieces, with none to deliver.

O LORD my God, if I have done this, if there is wrong in my hands,

if I have repaid my friend with evil or plundered my enemy without cause,

let the enemy pursue my soul and overtake it, and let him trample my life to the ground and lay my glory in the dust. Selah

Arise, O LORD, in your anger; lift yourself up against the fury of my enemies; awake for me; you have appointed a judgment.

Let the assembly of the peoples be gathered about you; over it return on high.

The LORD judges the peoples; judge me, O LORD, according to my righteousness and according to the integrity that is in me.

Oh, let the evil of the wicked come to an end, and may you establish the righteous—you who test the minds and hearts, O righteous God!

My shield is with God, who saves the upright in heart.

God is a righteous judge and a God who feels indignation every day.

If a man does not repent, God will whet his sword; he has bent and readied his bow;

he has prepared for him his deadly weapons, making his arrows fiery shafts.

Behold, the wicked man conceives evil is pregnant with mischief, and gives birth to lies.

He makes a pit, digging it out, and falls into the hole that he has made.

His mischief returns upon his own head, and on his own skull, his violence descends.

I will give to the LORD the thanks due to his righteousness, and I will sing praise to the name of the LORD, the Most High."

Although this spell requires some time to perform and originates from a Christian tradition, once you have crafted the elixir, its effects endure indefinitely. Simply keep the container with you wherever you go, and it will attract good fortune and happiness into your life.

A Protection Spell for Your Home

If you find yourself going through challenging times within your household, facing stress or emotional turmoil, or if the tranquility and harmony of your home are at risk, then you can greatly benefit from utilizing this enchantment.

Required Materials:

- A glass jar with a tightly sealed lid
- Fragments of glass

- Nail clippings, either from yourself or from an animal, such as your pet
- Small plugs
- Glass wool
- A thistle
- A quantity of Absinthe

Additionally, gather these elements that won't go inside the jar:

- A pentacle for banishment or red felt to craft one
- A consecrated black candle
- Banishing oil

Combine all the aforementioned ingredients within the glass jar and securely seal it. Position a banishment pentacle on the jar's lid. You can create a pentacle by cutting one out of red felt or using an existing one. Place the black candle, prepared with banishing oil, on top of the lid, right above the pentacle, and ignite the candle. Now, recite the following incantation:

"Black candle and ancient curses, unleash your powers, reverse the influence of previously cast spells, and leave pain and sorrow in the past."

Allow the candle to burn out completely. Once it does, take the jar and bury it in close proximity to your home. If performed with precision and sincere intent, you will experience a protective barrier surrounding your residence, which should endure for approximately six months. When the spell's potency starts to wane, simply repeat the process using a new jar.

A Potion for Prosperity

This spell offers potent magic for those seeking to enhance success in various aspects of life, such as career, personal goals, relationships, well-being, or any other area they wish to concentrate on.

The pursuit of peace and prosperity is a universal desire that comes into play in everyone's life at some point. With this option, you can attract the right intentions that may guide you towards achieving it.

Ingredients:

- A regular glass jar
- Three green and three gold candles
- Seven leaves each of rosemary, bay, basil, thyme, lavender, and clove
- Oil
- Three silver coins of any currency
- A wooden stick

The recipe for this potion is fairly straightforward. Combine all the herb leaves and coins in the jar, ensuring they are covered in oil. Create a circle around the jar with the candles, alternating between green and gold. Light the candles.

Using the wooden stick, stir the jar's contents clockwise for seven rotations while reciting the magic words. Repeat this set of phrases seven times: "Prosperity. Wealth. Abundance. Riches. Money. Fortune."

Now, stir the contents in the opposite direction and repeat the following set of phrases seven times: "Gold. Prosperity. Zenith. Manifest. Opulence."

Break the stick used for stirring in half and place it inside the jar. Leave the mixture within the candle circle and allow the candles to burn out. Once they have been extinguished, position the jar somewhere in your home to invite prosperity into your life.

A Potion for Relationships (For Love and Friendship)

Your relationships wield immense influence over your life's trajectory. In the grand scheme of human existence, it's often not merely your knowledge that shapes your journey and destination, but rather the individuals you're connected with. The presence of others can either propel you to greater heights or restrain your progress significantly. This is why crafting a concoction to attract love and companionship from the right people can hold such significance.

Ingredients:

- Rosewater
- Three ripe strawberries
- Three vanilla pods
- Three tablespoons of cocoa powder
- Three tablespoons of salt
- A saucepan
- A glass bottle
- A sheet of parchment paper
- A red marker pen

Begin by placing your saucepan on the stove and adding all the ingredients, excluding the paper, pen, and bottle. Allow them to simmer on low heat for approximately 30 minutes. While the mixture brews, take the parchment paper and inscribe the following words with your red marker:

"Pure love. Strong love. Open all the doors to me. Pure love. Strong friendship. May luck favor me."

Once done, roll the parchment paper and carefully insert it into the glass bottle. Afterward, strain the contents from the saucepan, pouring the infused rosewater liquid into the same bottle. Seal the bottle securely to prevent any spillage.

Hold the bottle in your hands and gently sway it back and forth while reciting the incantation you've written seven times.

A Potion for Cultivating Love from Someone

This may appear unconventional, but it's a potent spell with versatile applications. Initially designed to kindle affection in someone's heart towards you, it can be used for various reasons. One prominent use is when you desire someone to fall in love with you and yearn to be by your side. While this spell can indeed achieve that, I advise using it judiciously and responsibly. Moreover, it can be employed in different scenarios.

For instance, if your partner seems trapped in outdated perspectives, is stressed, or isn't attentive to your needs, they might lack the empathy and compassion required to maintain a balanced relationship. This spell can serve as a gentle reminder. If seeking forgiveness, it can influence their intentions positively.

Ingredients:

- A vial of salt
- A small lock of hair from the person you wish to resonate with the spell
- Nine candles in red, green, and yellow (nine of each)

Create a circle of salt large enough for you to sit comfortably within, positioning the candles around its perimeter. Alternate the candle colors around the circle, starting with green and progressing to yellow, red, and so forth.

Sit within the circle and meticulously light each candle one by one, commencing with the easternmost candle. Hold the lock of hair in your right hand, close your eyes, and repeat the person's name 99 times while visualizing them as vividly as possible in your mind's eye.

Allow the candles to burn out naturally and keep the lock of hair in your pillowcase for as long as you deem necessary.

Ishtar's Love Connection

To establish deep connections and foster love with those in your life, you can employ Ishtar's Love Ligament ritual. Ishtar, an ancient deity within Mesopotamian belief systems, was revered as both the goddess of warfare and passionate love. Employing this spell allows you to tap into the ancient essence of Ishtar, bringing love into your own life while invoking sentiments of love, empathy, and tranquility in others.

If you're seeking love in any aspect of your existence, this potent and enduring incantation can wield significant influence.

Ingredients:

• A piece of red silk ribbon measuring one meter in length.

For 48 consecutive nights, tie a single knot in the silk ribbon while reciting the following incantation:

"In the name of Ishtar, the one who nurtures all things to fruition, I bind you to me, and day by day, your love for me shall flourish like ivy upon the wall. So be it. So it shall come to pass."

On the 49th day, at daybreak, as the sun begins to grace the horizon, journey to a crossroads in a rural setting or a place intertwined with Hoodoo heritage, and set the ribbon ablaze, dispersing the ashes into the gentle breeze.

The Powerful Negra Cinta

I personally do not endorse the use of potent Black magic spells on others. However, individual circumstances can vary, and you may have your own reasons for considering such a spell. I am not here to pass judgment, but I strongly advise exercising extreme caution if you choose to proceed. I have included this spell for educational purposes only and will refrain from sharing others due to safety concerns.

The Negra Cinta is a formidable Black magic Hoodoo spell primarily intended for seeking revenge. In the early days of Hoodoo magic, Black individuals would employ this spell against those inflicting significant harm, such as slave owners or traders. It is a spell designed to redirect pain, trauma, and suffering back to those responsible. Nonetheless, it is an exceptionally challenging spell to perform due to the potent effects it can yield.

Ingredients:

- A black candle
- A sheet of rolling cigarette paper
- Scorpion oil (alacran oil)
- Snake fat
- A black pin and black ink
- A parrot feather
- A black ribbon or black belt
- Black salt
- Cemetery land or a location associated with Hoodoo origins

To ensure the correct execution of this spell, it is imperative to follow the steps precisely. Begin by carving the name of the person you intend to cast the spell on into the candle, using a knife or similar tool. Pour the scorpion oil over the engraving and sprinkle some black salt on it.

Allow the candle to stand upright for several hours before lighting it. Position a map of the person's geographical location next to the candle and jot down the wishes, requests, curses, or actions you desire to take against them. Ensure that you write these intentions with the parrot feather and black ink.

This is a critical part of the spell, so take great care in articulating your desires. You may aim to enlighten them about their wrongdoings, make them realize the extent of their cruelty, or wish for them to experience the pain they have caused—whatever you choose, inscribe it on the map.

Next, cover the map with the snake fat and leave the setup undisturbed until the candle has completely burned out. Following this, fold up the map and secure it with the black ribbon, tying the ribbon in a knot seven times. Seal the final knot with the black pin. As you tie each knot, recite the following passage seven times:

"Forces of malevolence, rulers of destinies since time immemorial, I invoke your immense strength to subdue every thought, word, and action of NN. May all misfortune befall them, may their cries go unheard, and may all the harm they've caused return to them and their family multiplied by a hundred. So shall it be."

Once the candle has been extinguished, gather the remnants along with your map, and wrap everything together using the ribbon and pin to secure the components. Finally, bury this bundle in a distant location within a cemetery. The spell will then begin to take effect as the magic starts to flow.

There is a wealth of resources and information available on other spells and possible incantations for you to explore. For now, you have a solid foundation to begin your journey and experiment with the capabilities of Hoodoo magic. Proceed with confidence, embark on this path, and uncover the wonders of Hoodoo's mystical power for yourself.

Conclusion

The fundamental concept underlying Hoodoo magic revolves around harnessing the inherent power residing within you, directing it in a constructive manner for your own benefit, and establishing a profound connection with the broader universe and its cosmic forces. It's vital to grasp that Hoodoo's influence extends across various facets of life, whether you seek to enhance your fortune, attain prosperity, foster peace, cultivate stronger relationships, or attain mental clarity.

In its essence, the heart of Hoodoo lies in the enhancement of your daily existence through focused intentions. This is accomplished by delving deep within yourself, tapping into your inner reservoir of strength, and embracing the energies of our ancestors and historical legacy. This practice holds immense potential, and even if you maintain skepticism initially, it's one of those disciplines that flourish over time. The more you engage in it, and the more receptive you become to the possibilities it offers, the more evident its impact becomes in your day-to-day life.

While this book serves as an introductory guide to get you started, the realm of Hoodoo magic extends far beyond the boundaries of our discussion. Once you've become well-acquainted with the foundational principles outlined in this book, you can embark on further explorations.

This entails delving into additional literature, particularly spell books, to gain deeper insights into what you can accomplish. It also involves immersing yourself in personal exploration of the practice, whether through documenting your experiences, engaging in meditation, or tuning into your inner emotions and instincts. There's a wealth of self-discovery awaiting you by looking within yourself. If you ever feel an instinctive urge to concoct a potion or cast a spell that aligns with your essence, and you sense the core of Hoodoo magic resonating within you, nudging you toward clarity, then more often than not, you should heed this inner calling.

Learn to trust your instincts; they can unveil the world to you. Remember, intentional thinking and the practice of Hoodoo magic can be an enriching and transformative journey. It has the potential to reshape your life, so it's crucial to treat the knowledge, your individual journey, and the experiences of others with utmost respect and care. Underestimating the profound insights you can glean from this path would be unwise.

For now, I conclude my message. I trust you found value in this book and gained some form of insight from its content. If you did, I would greatly appreciate hearing your thoughts. You can share your feedback by leaving a review on the platform where you acquired your copy. Your feedback holds immense significance to me, as it aids in my personal growth and striving for the best version of myself. I eagerly await your comments.

As you move forward, I extend my best wishes to you, particularly in your spiritual and magical pursuits. Good fortune be with you, and may your mind remain open to learning and the myriad new possibilities that accompany it. Until we meet again!